THEA BOWMAN

OTHER TITLES IN THIS SERIES

In My Own Words: Blessed Teresa of Calcutta

In My Own Words: Dorothy Day

In My Own Words: Henri Nouwen

In My Own Words: Joan Chittister

In My Own Words: Padre Pio

In My Own Words: Pope Benedict XVI

RELATED TITLES

*Sister Thea Bowman – Almost Home:
Living with Suffering and Dying DVD*

THEA BOWMAN

In My Own Words

Compiled and Edited by
Maurice J. Nutt, C.Ss.R.

Liguori

Imprimi Potest:
Thomas D. Picton, C.Ss.R.
Provincial, Denver Province
The Redemptorists

Published by Liguori Publications
Liguori, Missouri
www.liguori.org
To order, call 800-325-9521.

Library of Congress Cataloging-in-Publication Data

Bowman, Thea.
    Thea Bowman : in my own words / compiled and edited by Maurice J.
Nutt. -- 1st ed.
        p. cm. — (In my own words)
    ISBN 978-0-7648-1782-3
    1. Bowman, Thea. 2. African American Catholics—Religious life. 3.
Christian life—Catholic authors. I. Nutt, Maurice J. II. Title.
    BX4705.B8113A25 2009
    271'.97302—dc22
    [B]

                                                                    2008050899

Sources and permissions are listed at the end of the book.

Liguori Publications, a nonprofit corporation, is an apostolate of the
Redemptorists. To learn more about the Redemptorists, visit
Redemptorists.com.

Printed in the United States of America
20 19 18 / 5 4 3

Cover design: Jodi Hendrickson
Cover Photo: Gerard Pottebaum

townsfolk were a bit leery of the Franciscan sisters. They thought they worshipped statues and spoke in foreign tongues (Latin). However, while there was a sense of prejudice for Catholics in the deep South, the sisters soon won the people over by their dedication and assistance in meeting their urgent needs.

At age nine, Thea decided to become a Catholic. She admitted that it was not the theology or doctrine that drew her to the Catholic Church, but the example of how Catholics seemed to love and care for one another, most especially the poor and needy. Thea realized that religion was real and relevant: people put their faith into action. In 1953, at the age of fifteen, she told her family and friends she wanted to join the Franciscan
sisters. She left the familiar Mississippi terrain to venture off to the unfamiliar town of La Crosse, Wisconsin, where she would become the only African American member in the convent.

As a sister, Thea trained to become a teacher. She taught at all grade levels. However, her Franciscan superiors decided that Thea would be better suited as a college professor and, in 1968, sent her to The Catholic University of America in Washington, D.C., to earn her doctorate in English.

The turbulent decade of the 1960s was a period of transformation in a nation torn by racial strife and division. The rise of Dr. Martin Luther King, Jr., the Civil Rights Act, the march from Selma to Montgomery and the "Poor People's March" in Washington, D.C., the death of four young girls in a church in Birmingham, and the assassination of Dr. King in Memphis all challenged the country with a quest for justice and racial equality. The late '60s were also a time of transformation for Thea Bowman. Far away from the "old folks" and the down-home style of Canton, away from the solitude, sanctuary, and shelter of La Crosse, Wisconsin, it was in Washington, D.C., that Thea had both a spiritual and cultural awakening. In making vital contacts with the African American Catholic community in this large urban city, Thea found a soulful solace. The liturgical renewal of the Second Vatican Council encouraged Thea to discover her African American religious heritage and to enter her beloved Church fully functioning. It was also during this time that Thea delved deeper into the richness of her people's oral tradition as she studied English literature and linguistics that would shape her in sharing the songs of her people and proclaiming the anointed Word.

Thea earned her Ph.D. in English from The Catholic University of America in 1972 and spent the summer traveling through Europe and studying at Oxford University. She returned to La Crosse, Wisconsin, and started teaching English at Viterbo College. Professor Thea Bowman challenged her students to think for themselves. She believed that her students' opinions were just as valid as her opinions, as long as they could support them with evidence.

Thea was also in demand to share her gift of blackness in song and presentations on the college circuit. She emphasized that cultural awareness had, as a prerequisite, mutuality. She was eager to learn about the richness of other cultures, but also wanted to share the abundance of her African American culture.

In 1978, Thea returned home to Canton to care for her aging parents. It was during this time that she was appointed to direct the Office of Intercultural Affairs for the Diocese of Jackson. In this position, Thea continued to assail racial prejudice and promote cultural awareness and sensitivity. Thea's unequivocal vocation was to speak and write about the significance of black spirituality, black history and culture, black song, the black family, and on being black and Catholic.

The Institute for Black Catholic Studies (IBCS) was founded in 1980 at Xavier University of Louisiana in New Orleans. As a founding faculty member, Thea brought her indomitable spirit, engaging personality, and prophetic vision to the mission of the IBCS to provide an intellectual, spiritual, pastoral, and cultural immersion into the black Catholic experience. Thea taught courses in black literature, religion, and the arts; she also taught courses on the spirituals and preaching. Her students could attest that Thea's classes weren't just lectures—they were life-changing encounters.

The year 1984 brought many challenges for Thea Bowman. Both her parents died, and she was diagnosed with breast cancer. Her friends and students encouraged her to choose life. Thea vowed to "live until I die" and continued her rigorous schedule of speaking engagements. Even when it became increasingly difficult, as the cancer moved to her bones, Thea would not stop being a witness for the Lord. Clothed in her customary African garb, Thea would arrive in a wheelchair. She had lost her hair due to the chemotherapy treatments, but her big eyes were bright and she always wore a pleasant smile.

Thea did not let her wheelchair or the deterioration of her body keep her from one notable and unprecedented event—an opportunity to address the U.S. Catholic bishops at their annual June meeting held in 1989 at Seton Hall University in East Orange, New Jersey. Thea spoke to the bishops as a sister having a "heart-to-heart" conversation with her brothers. She had something very important to say to them, something that needed to be said. In this well crafted, yet at times quite spontaneous message, Thea spoke of the Church as her "home," as her "family of families," and about trying to find her way "home." She told them the "true truth" about what it means to be black and Catholic. She instructed and enlightened the bishops on African American history and spirituality. She challenged the bishops to continue to evangelize the African American community, to promote inclusivity and full participation of blacks within Church leadership, and to understand the necessity and value of Catholic schools in the African American community.

When she was through, she urged the bishops to move together, cross arms, and sing with her, "We Shall Overcome." She seemingly touched the hearts of the bishops, as evidenced by their thunderous applause and flowing tears.

Thea Bowman had the ability to communicate and relate to a wide range of people, from the neighbor next door to the high school student in the classroom. She offered love and compassion to those living with AIDS, enjoyed hearty laughter with the "old folks," entertained celebrities like Harry Belafonte and Whoopi Goldberg, intrigued the veteran CBS news reporter, Mike Wallace, provided encouragement for single mothers, and lectured the Roman Catholic hierarchy.

Sister Thea Bowman was many things to many people: one of the "old folks"; a devoted Franciscan religious woman; an advocate of all cultures, while maintaining love for "her own black self"; a proud maiden of Mississippi; a persuasive preacher; a tenacious teacher; a soul-stirring singer; a bold "true truth" teller; an instrument of peace, love, and joy; a lover of the Church; a faithful friend and spiritual mother to many.

Sister Thea Bowman never needed or wanted anyone to speak for her. So allow me, as her former student, to give you Thea Bowman, FSPA, in her own words: "The gift that has been given to me is the gift I share with you."

MAURICE J. NUTT, C.SS.R.

"GO DOWN MOSES"
The Wisdom of the "Old Folks"

When Israel was in Egypt's lan'
Let my people go.
Oppressed so hard they could not stan'
Let my people go.
Go down Moses way down in Egypt lan'
Tell ol' Pharaoh
Let my people go.

AFRICAN AMERICAN SPIRITUAL

I'm what they used to call an "old folks" child. When I was growing up, my parents, especially my mother, made a concerted effort to keep me in touch with the elders. She wanted me to hear from them. She wanted me to learn the old songs and the old stories. She wanted me to learn from their lips about slavery and what they had been through.

SR. THEA: HER OWN STORY

We were taught that the old people were the treasures of the people: they were the teachers, they were the preachers, they were the healers, and they were the lovers.

SR. THEA: HER OWN STORY

My mother wanted me to be sweet and cultured; she wanted a child who was going to be a little lady who would sit right and talk right, but instead she got a little "rowdy!"

SR. THEA: HER OWN STORY

My mother was born in Greenville, Mississippi, and her mother was a teacher, and she lived in an area where people were very, very poor but very, very proud. They valued learning, they valued music, and they valued the arts. My father was really dedicated to trying to help people, and I grew up with that example.

ALMOST HOME

God was so alive in my world. I was reared around a lot of old people. They knew Scripture. I knew people who could not read or write, but they could quote you a Scripture with the chapter and verse. They would use Scripture when they were tired and a Scripture when they were frustrated, a Scripture to challenge us…a Scripture to threaten you, a Scripture to reward you or to praise you or to teach you; I grew up in that kind of world.

ALMOST HOME

Old folks used to say, "God is bread when you're hungry. God is water when you're thirsty. God is a shelter from the storm. God is rest when you're weary. God's my doctor. God's my lawyer. God's my captain who never lost a battle. God is my lily of the valley."

ALMOST HOME

My mother and father would say, "they don't understand; if they hate you, return love for their hatred." I grew up in a community that said we must return love, no matter what.

INTERVIEW WITH JOE SMITH
WMTV, MADISON, WISCONSIN, 1988

I learned survival. I'm from Mississippi, and the people who did not learn to contain their anger and frustration did not live long. You learn very early on how to wear the mask so that if I had to work with you and I felt—not that I knew—that you were racist in your heart, I learned to guard my manner, to guard my speech, even to guard my thoughts, my feelings, passions, and emotions. I did that not because I hated you, but because I had to survive. I did that because my people had to have a job, because their children had to walk in safety.

INTERVIEW WITH JOE SMITH
WMTV, MADISON, WISCONSIN, 1988

As a child, I was taught that [if others chose to act with prejudice], that was their business, and we pray for them and speak of them with respect. Of course as a child, I didn't like that, and I thought my mother was crazy, but as I have grown up I understood what she was trying to do. She was saying as I hate, I don't care what the reason, if I hate, the hate eats into my heart and eats into my soul. And I can be a loving person and caring person—that doesn't mean I'm supposed to take abuse, but it means that I have to try to have an understanding heart and understand how they were raised and understand that somehow they need help.

SR. THEA: HER OWN STORY

When I was growing up, many of the old women who had undergone the ignominy of slavery were around, and they told us about slavery because they said we had to know about freedom. They told us about misery. The black woman has a task when the world says to her children, when the world says to her husband, when the world says to her mamma and to her, "There's something wrong with you. Your skin is too black. Your nose is too flat. Your hair is too nappy and too short. And you're slow. And you're ignorant. And you can't learn like white folks. And you're immoral." That's what the racist society told us and told our children about themselves. The result was one of the great problems of the black community, the problem of low self-esteem, and it kills us.

"EXPERIENCING BLACK SPIRITUALITY:
FLYING WITH THE METAPHOR"
SECOND CONFERENCE ON THE SPIRITUAL WOMAN,
MERCY COLLEGE OF DETROIT, 1989

I'm an "old folks" child, and I never realized until I was grown up how well they taught me values, how well they taught me survival skills: how to face life, how to face pain, how to face death, how not to be scared, and if you're scared that don't make no difference, just as long as you keep on steppin'.

SR. THEA: HER OWN STORY

I grew up with people who taught us how to respect and appreciate nature, to study nature's secrets, to reverence the very soil beneath our feet. My people in the South were farmers and they learned patience. You can't rush the seasons; you can't call forth the rain.

They also learned not to waste! And that's something we all need to pay more attention to today! It's important not to take more than we need. Take your share and leave the rest for the others. If we live cooperatively the earth produces sufficiently to feed and shelter us all.

"TRUSTING THE PROPHETIC CALL,"
CREATION MAGAZINE

The old ladies say that if you love the Lord with your whole heart, then your whole soul and your whole mind and all your strength, then you praise the Lord with your whole heart and soul and mind and strength and you don't bring him any feeble service.

"TO BE BLACK AND CATHOLIC"
ADDRESS TO THE U.S. CATHOLIC BISHOPS, JUNE 1989

Old folks taught us that we have a responsibility, you have an obligation to help, you have an obligation to build your community, and you have an obligation to pay back. Old lady said, "I'm gonna help you because you need some help, and when you get able, I don't want you to pay me back, then you help somebody. When you help somebody, that's how you become big, that's how you become proud, not by getting things but by helping somebody and leaving the world better than you found it.

SR. THEA: HER OWN STORY

The gift you have becomes a gift to humanity.

INTERVIEW WITH JOE SMITH
WMTV, MADISON, WISCONSIN, 1988

"Got a Home in That Rock"
The Black Family

I've got a home in a-that Rock.
Don't you see? Don't you see?
I've got a home in a-that Rock.
Don't you see? Don't you see?
Between the earth and sky,
thought I heard my Savior cry,
I've got a home in a-that Rock.
Don't you see?

AFRICAN AMERICAN SPIRITUAL

If we are not family, we can't become Church.

FAMILIES: BLACK AND CATHOLIC,
CATHOLIC AND BLACK

This book...assumes that the Black family is alive and well. It assumes further that we as a people need to find ways old and new to walk and talk together; to bond more surely; to extend family more widely and effectively, so that no one is fatherless, motherless, sisterless, or brotherless; so that no one lacks the life-sustaining human support of family.

FAMILIES: BLACK AND CATHOLIC,
CATHOLIC AND BLACK

Too often, [other] people come to us with answers to our problems. They don't bother to try to find out who we are, how we think, and what we're about. Too often, people who come to help do not realize that black family is alive and well and that even when broken, even when hurting, it fosters deep faith and forges strong bonds.

FAMILIES: BLACK AND CATHOLIC,
CATHOLIC AND BLACK

Everybody needs family. We start with a basic human need for family and for one another. We realize that one father, one mother are not enough: that families need the support of other families, and so we seek ways of bonding, nourishing, and healing.

We become community when families share values and needs. This bonding strengthens and nourishes us. The love that makes us community also makes us truly Church.

FAMILIES: BLACK AND CATHOLIC,
CATHOLIC AND BLACK

We all have multi-cultural people in our families. Just look round this room, all kinds of beauty. We need to know the histories and cultures from which we come, to claim all, to use all, all the experience, all the survival and coping mechanisms, all that we need if we're going to get over to that Promised Land, to the new Jerusalem, where there won't be anybody hungry, or lonely or poor, because we're walking together as brothers and sisters in Jesus' Name.

"BLACK HISTORY AND CULTURE"
U.S. CATHOLIC HISTORIAN

We must recognize who we are and how we are and celebrate, because in our history and in our culture we find power. Do you remember the old days when we were out in the fields telling the stories and singing the songs? Some of you never experienced that reality, but that's a part of our history, too. Listening to grown-ups talk on city stoops, or around the family table, or in the message of the Gospel preacher, we heard the stories of our people. The knowledge of their life and culture was power, spirit-power, faith-power, health and healing-power, life-power, love-power. Some of us no longer take time to be together as families and as the families of families which make Church. We no longer have the time or inclination to tell the stories, to pray the prayers or sing the songs, or share the jokes and anecdotes, to shuck and jive and play together, to pass on the old coping mechanisms and survival techniques. We have to get the extra dollar or watch TV. We don't have time to share history and culture.

"BLACK HISTORY AND CULTURE"
U.S. CATHOLIC HISTORIAN

A disproportionate number of black people are poor. Poverty, deprivation, discrimination, stunted physical, intellectual and spiritual growth—I don't need to tell you this, but I want to remind you, more than a third of the black people that live in the United States live in poverty, the kind of poverty that lacks basic necessity.

I'm talking about old people who have worked hard all their lives and don't have money for adequate food or shelter or medical care.

I'm talking about children who can never have equal access and equal opportunity because poverty doomed them to low birth weight and retardation and unequal opportunity for education.

More than 55 percent of black babies are born to single mothers. About 41 percent of black families are single-parent families headed by women. The divorce rate for blacks is twice as high as for whites.

Black children are twice as likely as white children to be born prematurely, to suffer from low birth weight, to live in substandard housing, to have no parent employed.

Unemployment and underemployment among us are endemic. And many of us don't have the social and political contacts that put us where the jobs are when jobs are being passed out. One of every 21 black males is murdered. A disproportionate number of our men are dying of suicide and AIDS and drug abuse and low self-esteem.

"TO BE BLACK AND CATHOLIC"
ADDRESS TO THE U.S. CATHOLIC BISHOPS, JUNE 1989

Stress

Loneliness frustration worry
Anxiety obsession oppression
Repression depression bills inflation
Insecurity poverty unemployment underemployment
Layoffs rip-offs last-hired first-fired
Injustice unequal opportunity
Systematic exclusion from full participation in political,
social, educational, economic, and
religious organizations and institutions
inadequate education inadequate housing
homelessness inadequate health care
inadequate sanitation inadequate nutrition
retardation senility starvation aggression
violence crime murder rape robbery incest conflict
economic conflict religious conflict family conflict
crime black-on-black crime jail
imprisonment police brutality violence
family violence child abuse wife abuse husband abuse
teen-age pregnancies unwanted pregnancies
abortion frustration alcohol abuse drug abuse
chemical dependency illness accident hypochondria
dependency agency dependency delinquency
street gangs rumbles wars
drop-outs cop-outs run-aways
hustlers dealers pimping
prostitution
separation death suicide

mobility upward mobility
materialism consumerism
elitism classism racism sexism
manipulation exploitation
anxiety loneliness
stress

"THE CHALLENGES"
FAMILIES: BLACK AND CATHOLIC,
CATHOLIC AND BLACK

Traditions and rituals that embody…faith, values,
and love have to be worked on, and so we have family
histories, memories, prayer, and catechesis, and celebra-
tions as well as family dreams, goals, and plans. In faith
we remember our history; we remember that we've
come this far by faith. We celebrate that faith in our
liturgies. We pass on our values when we dream and
plan and work together. We celebrate the love we bear
for one another in family fun, being together, enjoying
one another, and in family ministry. We minister to
our family, we minister within our family, we minister
within the Black community. We, as Church, minister
to our brothers and sisters, wherever we find them.

FAMILIES: BLACK AND CATHOLIC,
CATHOLIC AND BLACK

Families
giving life
nurturing, nourishing
supporting, sustaining
encoding values
breaking bread
giving
forgiving

Black Families
understanding our
black history
treasuring our
black heritage
rejoicing to be who
we are
teaching black values to
black children in
black ways
living, loving, talking, walking
shucking, jiving, laughing
playing, dancing, singing
thinking, doing as
black folks
can and do

Black Catholic Families
worshiping the Lord with
heart and soul
sharing bread and Eucharist
strengthening family unity
through Faith and
Sacrament
witnessing the Good News of
Christ the Liberator
working to bring about
the coming of
the Kingdom
feeding the hungry
sheltering the homeless
walking in solidarity with
the oppressed and poor
signaling the eschatological
reality of God's
love
challenging one another and
challenging the
CHURCH to be
truly Christian
truly Catholic

FAMILIES: BLACK AND CATHOLIC,
CATHOLIC AND BLACK

"TELL THEM I'M A CHILD OF GOD"
The Giftedness of Children

If anybody ask you, who I am?
Who I am? Who I am?
If anybody ask you, who I am?
Tell them I'm a child of God.

AFRICAN AMERICAN SPIRITUAL

Children close to the heart of Family, Community, Church respond and remain constant to the values of Family, Community, Church.

FAMILIES: BLACK AND CATHOLIC,
CATHOLIC AND BLACK

What we say to our children is: You have to be bi-cultural, you have to be multicultural, you have to learn many ways, many styles. You have to be adaptable if you want to survive.

You have to adapt your speech, you have to adapt your dress, you have to adapt your manner, you have to adapt your ways of thinking, and it gives us flexibility.

I ask this question: Would you rather for your children to know one language or to know many?

When I am with my friends from Vietnam, I have to act in a different way than I act with my friends from Mississippi; that's the beauty of life.

INTERVIEW WITH JOE SMITH
WMTV, MADISON, WISCONSIN, 1988

If our children are to be adequately prepared for life in a pluralistic, multiethnic, multicultural world, they must learn to understand and appreciate the basic religious traditions of the persons with whom they live and work. When we as Catholic students, parents, faculty, staff, administrators, approach believers of other religious traditions with appreciation and reverence we realize their faith and faithfulness. We are inspired by their convictions. We are broadened by their perspectives and challenged by their questions. We learn from their religious experience. As we work with them for peace and justice, as we cooperate with them in feeding the hungry, clothing the naked, teaching the ignorant, empowering the oppressed, we truly share the Good News of the Kingdom.

"RELIGIOUS AND CULTURAL VARIETY:
GIFT TO CATHOLIC SCHOOLS"
THE NON-CATHOLIC IN THE CATHOLIC SCHOOL

The presence of persons (students, parents, teachers) from the variety of religious and cultural traditions within the close community of the Catholic school can provide for all our children from their earliest years a supportive environment in which to grow in mutual understanding as well as the opportunity for true ecumenical dialogue and collaboration on an on-going basis....

"RELIGIOUS AND CULTURAL VARIETY:
GIFT TO CATHOLIC SCHOOLS"
THE NON-CATHOLIC IN THE CATHOLIC SCHOOL

The poor are still trying to deal with a rising teenage pregnancy rate, single parentage where children are not supported by the total family, total community. You know how it was in the old days. If a child had a baby, the child's family and the community would intervene, because a child can't raise a child, and how can you...?

"MARTIN LUTHER KING:
SEIZE THE VISION" CELEBRATION
MILWAUKEE, WISCONSIN, 1988

I love teaching. I like children. I think they are much more fun than adults. In a remarkable sort of way, children will believe you if you tell them your truth. Not that you have a corner on the truth, but if you tell them your truth, there's that intuitive grasp that children will believe you. If you love them, they will let you love them. I'm attracted to the freshness and beauty of young people. It is so important that they learn to value themselves before the world has had a chance to beat them down.

INTERVIEW WITH JOE SMITH
WMTV, MADISON, WISCONSIN, 1988

I think that children carry a message just by the way they are, and it is a message that needs to be heard.

INTERVIEW WITH MIKE WALLACE
"60 MINUTES," CBS, 1987

Black is beautiful. You have to believe it. Should I try it out on Mike Wallace?

Black is beautiful, and then you take your finger and point it at yourself and say, "I am beautiful." And some children have a hard time saying that. When I say that I am beautiful, what does that mean? It means I am caring. It means I respect myself. It means I am confident. I am poised, and you go through all that....I still didn't hear Mike Wallace say black is beautiful. [Mike Wallace: "Black is beautiful!"] Amen!

INTERVIEW WITH MIKE WALLACE
"60 MINUTES," CBS, 1987

When I first found out I had cancer, I dealt with it with the children. Children could talk with me about issues and what was happening in their families. If their mother had cancer, they were asking all the questions they would have liked to ask their mothers. I would say to the child, go talk to your mother. She needs to hear your questions, and she needs to talk to you, and you could help her. She'll feel better, because she knows you're worried and she knows you care, and it would make it easier for both of you.

ALMOST HOME

To affirm the child because of his own worth; to look at the child and love the child and tell the child, "If anybody asks you who you are, just tell them you're a child of God. I may be poor, but I am somebody. My mama might be on drugs, but I am somebody. My daddy might be in jail, but I am somebody. You might think I'm slow, but I am somebody. I'm God's child."

SR. THEA: HER OWN STORY

"WALK TOGETHER CHILDREN"
On Being Church

❧

Walk together children and don't you get weary.
Walk together children and don't you get weary.
Walk together children and don't you get weary.
There's a great camp meeting in the Promised Land.

AFRICAN AMERICAN SPIRITUAL

I'm a pilgrim in the journey looking for home, and Jesus told me the church is my home, and Jesus told me that heaven is my home and I have here no lasting city. Cardinals, archbishops, bishops: My brothers or church, please help me to get home.

"TO BE BLACK AND CATHOLIC"
ADDRESS TO THE U.S. CATHOLIC BISHOPS, JUNE 1989

I was drawn to examine and accept the Catholic faith because of the day-to-day lived witness of Catholic Christians who first loved me, then shared with me their story, their values, their beliefs; who first loved me, then invited me to share with them in community, prayer and mission. As a child I did not recognize evangelization at work in my life. I did recognize love, service, community, prayer and faith.

"RELIGIOUS AND CULTURAL VARIETY:
GIFT TO CATHOLIC SCHOOLS"
THE NON-CATHOLIC IN THE CATHOLIC SCHOOL

The popes have said that "the home is the domestic Church": that we are the Church.….Family feeds the Church and [the] Church necessarily feeds family. If we're not Church at home, we can't be Church when we go to church. If we are not family, we can't become Church.

FAMILIES: BLACK AND CATHOLIC,
CATHOLIC AND BLACK

You know as well as I do that some of the best preaching does not go on in the pulpit, but as a Catholic Christian I have a responsibility to preach and to teach, to worship and to pray. Black folk can't just come into church and depend on the preacher and say, "Let Father do it." And if Father doesn't do it right, then they walk out and they complain, you know, "That liturgy didn't do anything for me."

The question that we raise is, what did you do for the liturgy? And the Church is calling us to be participatory and to be involved. The Church is calling us to feed and to clothe and to shelter and to teach. Your job is to enable me, to enable God's people, black people, white people, brown people, all the people, to do the work of the Church in the modern world. Teaching, preaching, witnessing, worshipping, serving, healing and reconciling...

"TO BE BLACK AND CATHOLIC"
ADDRESS TO THE U.S. CATHOLIC BISHOPS, JUNE 1989

I see people who are well educated and experienced and willing to work. Sometimes they're religious; sometimes they're lay. They are not included in the initial stages of planning. They are not included in the decision making. Now, I know you are bishops and I'm not talking about somebody coming into your diocese and trying to tell you what to do. I'm talking about the normal, church-authorized consultative process that attempts to enable the people of God to be about the work of the Catholic Church. If you know what I'm talking about, say "Amen."

"TO BE BLACK AND CATHOLIC"
ADDRESS TO THE U.S. CATHOLIC BISHOPS, JUNE 1989

To what extent are you ready to eat, to pray, to play, to work with the people of the universe? And if you haven't got time to play with us, to put your feet under the table and rest yourself a while, it is unlikely that you can share faith, life, and love with us. Jesus had time to spend at the wedding feast. He and his disciples were there because it was important to be there....

"COSMIC SPIRITUALITY: NO NEUTRAL GROUND"
1987 NATIONAL CONGRESS OF THE
RELIGIOUS FORMATION CONFERENCE

The old lady says, "I go to church, and I lay my burden at the door. I know I'm going to pick it up again, but I come to church because I need me some rest, and I need me some strength." And the young man says, "I got to get my batteries recharged."

Do you feel the energy in this church? The energy is power—it's power to heal, power to give life, to sustain life, it's even power to restore life.

"HEALING MINISTRY"
ST. STEPHEN'S CATHOLIC CHURCH, MINNEAPOLIS, 1989

We are the Catholic Church. The majority of people in the Catholic Church are people of color. There are more Catholics [elsewhere] right now than in North America. There are more Catholics in South America than in Eastern Europe. The complexion of the College of Cardinals, the complexion of the hierarchy has changed....

So when my Native American brothers and sisters praise the Lord, they respond to the Great Spirit; they attempt to live in harmony with that Great Spirit within the Catholic Church and to share the wisdom of their ancestry with those of us who are not so blessed.

My Hispanic brothers and sisters have an ancient tradition of religious education that takes place in the home, in the neighborhood, in the community....and they attempt to share that with the whole Catholic Church.

You hear the Latin American bishops speak out, you hear the African bishops speak out, you hear Cardinal Sin speak out, and their different voices claiming one Lord, one faith, one baptism, one Church. In the meantime, so many people misinterpret the universality of the Church. They tried to tell us that to be universal was to be all the same.

INTERVIEW WITH JOE SMITH
WMTV, MADISON, WISCONSIN, 1988

Catholic Christians come into my community, and they helped us with education, they helped us with health care, they helped us to find our self-respect and to realize our capabilities when the world had told us for so long that we were nothing and would amount to nothing. And I wanted to be a part of that effort. That's radical Christianity, that's radical Catholicism. How do we find the needs of God's people? How do we as a Catholic Christian community of believers say that we believe that God is active in our lives, and we want to share the Good News we have found with you?

Interview With Joe Smith
WMTV, Madison, Wisconsin, 1988

What's Good News when you are hungry? What's Good News when you can't read? And what's Good News when you can't find a job? And what's Good News when you are lonely and weary and you come together in Jesus' name to celebrate what Catholics say is the central act of our religion, which is Eucharist? And how can you and I celebrate Eucharist together, if we do not care about each other outside of the Church?

When we do these things, then the Catholic Church ministers to us and we as Catholic Christians minister to one another. And we do that in community with the Holy Father, in community with our archbishops and bishops and the priests, the religious and the little children.

Interview With Joe Smith
WMTV, Madison, Wisconsin, 1988

It was not liturgy that drew me. It was not theology or doctrine (I didn't know anything about that); it was the witness of Catholic Christians who were really making a difference in people's lives that made me interested in the Catholic Church.

INTERVIEW WITH JOE SMITH
WMTV, MADISON, WISCONSIN, 1988

I have to assume the responsibility of reaching out to my sisters and my brothers, and as I reach out, I take my friends with me. I introduce my friends to my friends. We begin to work together being Church. We are the Church!

INTERVIEW WITH JOE SMITH
WMTV, MADISON, WISCONSIN, 1988

When we come together in Jesus' name to do the work of the Church, when we come together as Church to worship and praise, to preach and to teach, to feed the hungry, to clothe the naked, to teach the children, to help the brother who has AIDS, to try to deal with the children who are being coerced to sell drugs, when we reach out to the lonely and the alienated and the afflicted, when we help the old folks, we don't realize that we are the Church and we are doing the work of the Church.

SR. THEA: HER OWN STORY

Can you see yourself in a church where there are people who are black, where there are people who are white, where there are people who are brown, where there are people who are of Asian heritage and people of Australian heritage and people of Native heritage? Where we all come together really being ourselves and sharing our sorrows and our joys, sharing our goals and our determinations? How rich we would be!

SR. THEA: HER OWN STORY

I can be a bridge over troubled water. I can take you by the hand and take you with me into the black community. I can walk you into your community, and if I walk with you into your community, I don't enter as a stranger, I walk as your sister.

SR. THEA: HER OWN STORY

Today we're called to walk together in a new way toward that land of promise, and to celebrate who we are and whose we are. If we as Church walk together, don't let nobody separate you. That's one thing black folk can teach you. Don't let folk divide you or put the lay folk over here and the clergy over here, put the bishops in one room and the clergy in the other room, put the women over here and the men over here.

The Church teaches us that the Church is a family. It is a family of families, and the families got to stay together. We know that if we do stay together, if we walk and talk and work and play and stand together in Jesus' name, we'll be who we say we are, truly Catholic; and we shall overcome—overcome the poverty, overcome the loneliness, overcome the alienation and build together a holy city, a new Jerusalem, a city set apart where they'll know we are his because we love one another.

"TO BE BLACK AND CATHOLIC"
ADDRESS TO THE U.S. CATHOLIC BISHOPS, JUNE 1989

May the Spirit within us and among us inspire us to keep on keeping on, in our homes and families, in our communities and in our Church. May the Spirit inspire us and may we share our spiritual and cultural gifts with the Church and with the world. We've come this far by faith. Can't turn around.

"BLACK HISTORY AND CULTURE"
U.S. CATHOLIC HISTORIAN

"GIVE ME THAT OLD TIME RELIGION"
On Being Black and Catholic

Give me that old time religion.
Give me that old time religion.
Give me that old time religion.
It's good enough for me.

AFRICAN AMERICAN SPIRITUAL

On this historic occasion of the Fifth National Black Catholic Congress, we have come from all over the country, from the Islands, and from Africa saying, "we want to know more about ourselves, we want to look deeply into our past and touch the fabric of our being, for we know that when we know our history and our culture, we are fortified as individuals and as a people. When we know ourselves, we bring the gift of our history and our culture to one another, to the Church, and to the world. We sing, "My soul looks back and wonders how I got over." *My soul looks back*—I learn and claim my history. *My soul wonders how I got over*—I investigate and embrace the spiritual and psychological survival skills embodied in my culture.

"BLACK HISTORY AND CULTURE"
U.S. CATHOLIC HISTORIAN

Our history includes the services of a Simon of Cyrene, the search of that Ethiopian eunuch; the contributions of Black Egypt in art, mathematics, monasticism, and politics; the art and architecture of Zimbabwe; the scholarship of Timbuktu; the dignity and serenity of textile, gold work, and religion in Ghana; the pervasive spirituality and vitality of Nigeria; the political and social systems of Zaire.

Our history includes enslavement, oppression and exploitation. As Malcolm X phrased it, "Our people didn't come here on the Mayflower." Many of them came in slave ships, in chains.

"BLACK HISTORY AND CULTURE"
U.S. CATHOLIC HISTORIAN

Culture is the expression whereby we as the family of Christian, black Catholic people learn from our history and accept it all. We have to stop fussing and fighting about who's too yellow, and who's not Creole, who came from what island, and how much money or education or influence it takes to belong to this or that. We are a multi-cultural people. We must claim our roots and proclaim our peace.

"BLACK HISTORY AND CULTURE"
U.S. CATHOLIC HISTORIAN

I walk in a number of different communities, just like my Native American brothers and sisters and my Hispanic brothers and sisters, my Asian brothers and sisters; we have to walk in more than one world. When I come into the world of academe, or when I come into the world of business, or when I come into the world of politics or statesmanship, or into the world of international conversation, I have to be bilingual, bicultural. I have to be able to talk your talk and talk it better than you can, if I am going to be accepted and respected by many people in your society.

INTERVIEW WITH JOE SMITH
WMTV, MADISON, WISCONSIN, 1988

When we know who we are and claim the history, we claim the struggle, the pain, the challenge, the purpose, the journey, and the dream. We are who we are and whose we are because of all our journeys, and the children that belong to our communities are enriched because of a pluralism that reflects life in a world that is pluralistic. Do we know all we can know, of ourselves, of our history, of our arts, and of our experience, of our goals and of our values, the full range of what has made us a people. When we know and understand, then we can do what we need to do to help ourselves.

"BLACK HISTORY AND CULTURE"
U.S. CATHOLIC HISTORIAN

Where black culture and spirituality are alive and well in our hearts and homes and neighborhoods, we bring them easily and joyfully into our churches. Where black culture is alive in our churches, its vitality spills over into our communities. It becomes a source of energy and vitality.

Some of us say we don't need black culture. We're comfortable. Do you hear me? Are you with me? I'm from Mississippi. I don't know how to deal with a quiet audience.

"BLACK HISTORY AND CULTURE"
U.S. CATHOLIC HISTORIAN

When we as delegates to the National Black Catholic Congress live and celebrate our history and our culture, we will address concerns that many black Catholics express and that are reflected in the working documents of this National Black Catholic Congress. When we understand our history and culture, then we can develop the ritual, the music, and the devotional expression that satisfy us in church. We can develop the cognitive-based religious education and the catechesis that will speak to the hearts of our people. We can develop the systems of service that respect us, who we are, how we operate as a people, and how our families really are. And we can bring new life.

"BLACK HISTORY AND CULTURE"
U.S. CATHOLIC HISTORIAN

I'm from Mississippi. The first schools in Mississippi were started in the cathedral basement by diocesan priests and a group of lay women. For so many of us, being black and Catholic means having come into the church because education opened the door to evangelization. It means, in an age when black men and black women were systematically kept out of the priesthood and out of most religious communities, there were those who cared and who came and who worked with and for us and among us and helped us to help ourselves.

And now our black American bishops, in the name of the Church universal, have publicly declared that we as a people of faith, as a Catholic people of God, have come of age. And it is time for us to be evangelizers of ourselves.

"To Be Black and Catholic"
Address to the U.S. Catholic Bishops, June 1989

What does it mean to be black and Catholic? It means that I come to my church fully functioning. That doesn't frighten you, does it? I come to my church fully functioning. I bring myself, my black self, all that I am, all that I have, all that I hope to become, I bring my whole history, my traditions, my experience, my culture, my African American song and dance and gesture and movement and teaching and preaching and healing and responsibility as gifts to the church.

"To Be Black and Catholic"
Address to the U.S. Catholic Bishops, June 1989

To be black and Catholic means to realize that the work of the ordained ministers is not a threat to me, and I'm no threat to that. The work of the ordained minister, of the professional minister, is to enable the people of God to do the work of the Church. To feed sacramentally, to enable us to preach and to teach, and I ain't necessarily talking preaching in the pulpit.

"To Be Black and Catholic"
Address to the U.S. Catholic Bishops, June 1989

The majority of priests, religious, and lay ministers who serve the black community in the United States still are not from the black community, and many of those people who attempt to serve among us, some of them perhaps in your diocese, do not feel an obligation to learn or understand black history and spirituality or culture or life, black tradition or ritual. They work for the people, but they have not learned to share life and love and laughter with the people. They somehow insulate themselves from the real lives of the people, because they don't feel comfortable with black people.

"TO BE BLACK AND CATHOLIC"
ADDRESS TO THE U.S. CATHOLIC BISHOPS, JUNE 1989

I travel all over the country, and I see it: black people within the Church, black priests, sometimes even black bishops, who are invisible. And when I say that, I mean they are not consulted. They are not included. Sometimes decisions are made that affect the black community for generations, and they are made in rooms by white people behind closed doors.

Some of us are poor. Some of us have not had the advantages of education. But how can people still have a voice and a role in the work of the Church? Isn't that what the Church is calling us all to?

"TO BE BLACK AND CATHOLIC"
ADDRESS TO THE U.S. CATHOLIC BISHOPS, JUNE 1989

Black people who are still victims within the church of paternalism, of a patronizing attitude, black people who within the church have developed a mission mentality—they don't feel called, they don't feel responsible, they don't do anything. Let Father do it, let the sisters do it, let the friends and benefactors from outside do it. That's the mission mentality. And it kills us, and it kills our churches. And so, within the Church, how can we work together so that all of us have equal access to input, equal access to opportunity, equal access to participation?

Go into a room and look around and see who's missing, and send some of your folks out to call them in so that the Church can be what she claims to be, truly Catholic.

"TO BE BLACK AND CATHOLIC"
ADDRESS TO THE U.S. CATHOLIC BISHOPS, JUNE 1989

Catholic schools have been a primary instrument of evangelization within the black community. The Church has repeatedly asked black folk, "What do you want, what can the church do for you? And black folk all over the country are saying, "Help us with education." We need education. The way out of poverty is through education.

"TO BE BLACK AND CATHOLIC"
ADDRESS TO THE U.S. CATHOLIC BISHOPS, JUNE 1989

I like being black. I have friends who are white and brown and yellow and red—all the colors in between. I love being with my friends, and I love sharing with them, but I love being myself. And I thank God for making me my black self.

SR. THEA: HER OWN STORY

Let's remember the ones who brought us this far in faith, who led us and fed us in faith: St. Simon of Cyrene and the Ethiopian eunuch, Anthony of Egypt, Cyril of Alexandria, Moses the Black, Martin de Porres, Charles Lwanga and the Ugandan martyrs, Frederick Douglass, Harriet Tubman, Sojourner Truth, Henriette Delille, Augustus Tolton, George Washington Carver, Booker T. Washington, W.E.B. DuBois, Mary Church Terrell, Marian Anderson, Paul Robeson, Langston Hughes, Jackie Robinson, Rosa Parks, Medgar Evers, Malcolm X, Martin Luther King, Jr., Andrew Young, James Baldwin, Desmond Tutu, the black Catholic bishops, all the priests, sisters, teachers, preachers and leaders, all the fathers and mothers, grandparents and great-grands, adoptive parents, godparents, play parents, brothers, sisters, husbands, wives, friends, neighbors, lovers, and children.

"BLACK HISTORY AND CULTURE"
U.S. CATHOLIC HISTORIAN

Black Catholics

Christians baptized in Christ Jesus and
   guided by His Spirit
united in faith and worship
sharing Sacraments
living signs of His living presence in our world
building up His Body
continuing His Sacred Mission as prophet—
   proclaiming God's Word
priest—celebrating, worshipping
servant—ministering to the peoples of the world
witnessing (together with the Holy Father, bishops,
priests and deacons, lay men and women
   and children everywhere)
that God is love.

FAMILIES: BLACK AND CATHOLIC,
CATHOLIC AND BLACK

"A LITTLE TALK WITH JESUS"
The Power of Prayer

O a little talk with Jesus makes it right, all right,
Little talk with Jesus makes it right, all right,
Troubles of ev'ry kind,
Thank God I'll always find
That a little talk with Jesus makes it right.

AFRICAN AMERICAN SPIRITUAL

Our old folks would go to church and pray, and they'd come home happy. Within the traditional prayer of the black community, there were ways of controlling the mind, the mood and even the body, and doing it in Jesus' name. I thank God for the gift of my people....

Our prayer tradition attempts to go to God with feeling and passion and emotion and intensity. I want to be a part of what Jesus felt as he hung on the cross. I want to feel the anguish. I want to feel the love that motivated him to save us. He's the Almighty Word who leapt down from heaven. He's the son of the eternal father who became human like us in all things save sin. Yet, he accepted the sufferings of a lifetime as a human being to give us life. I want to feel that love, that compassion....

"LORD, LET ME LIVE TILL I DIE,"
PRAYING MAGAZINE

I did not realize I was receiving a religious education—that I was being taught prayer, salvation history, morals and values, faith, hope, love, and joy. I did not realize that the songs would form the basis of my lifelong religious education and the catalyst that would impel me to seek books and classes, exegesis and explication...in my eagerness to know and understand more of the Words of Salvation. I did not know that I was being taught modes of prayer that would increasingly enrich my personal prayer, community prayer, liturgical

prayer; modes of prayer that I have been privileged to
share with my brothers, sisters, and children of diverse
races and culture, economic backgrounds, and religions.

SISTER THEA: SONGS OF MY PEOPLE

I don't think it starts in church. I think it starts
outside of church when we love one another, when we
become friends and we can walk hand in hand into
the house of the Lord and celebrate. But to me to pray
together when our hearts are not one, when we are not
at least trying to bridge the gaps, is sacrilege.

SR. THEA: HER OWN STORY

Each spiritual is in its own way a prayer—of yearning or celebration, of praise, petition, or contemplation,
a simple lifting of heart, mind, voice, and life to God.

SISTER THEA: SONGS OF MY PEOPLE

People come because they want to be with me and
they want to help [as the cancer progresses]. I tell them
if you want to help, why don't you sit with me, just be
with me or please pray with me?

ALMOST HOME

We have come together in Jesus' name and we pray, Oh Father, give us the spirit of transformation that the water of our lives may become purest wine and that your glory may be revealed to all the brothers and sisters, to the whole cosmos, to the limits of the universe. God's glory is revealed because we love one another across the barriers and boundaries of race, culture, and class. We love not just in words but in food and in prayer and in song and dance and in learning and working together.

Let the church say *Amen.*

"COSMIC SPIRITUALITY: NO NEUTRAL GROUND"
1987 NATIONAL CONGRESS OF THE
RELIGIOUS FORMATION CONFERENCE

We have to take time to listen to God in Scripture, in nature, in our own heart, in our feelings, passions, and dreams. We have to listen to each other….We have to take the *time* to listen and observe. We have to take the time to pray and dialogue together, no matter how poor, hurting, or weak we are. Then we can begin to effect change *here and now!*

"TRUSTING THE PROPHETIC CALL,"
CREATION MAGAZINE

If we are to serve, if we are to care, if we are to minister, we have to get right inside. And so let us pray: Spirit, touch me. Touch me with your grace. Touch me with your wisdom. Touch me with your love so that I can help somebody, so that I can serve somebody, so that I can bless somebody. Be the bridge over troubled waters so that I can be the balm in Gilead, be the hands of Jesus stretched out to heal.

"HEALING MINISTRY"
ST. STEPHEN'S CATHOLIC CHURCH, MINNEAPOLIS, 1989

Let us resolve to make this week holy by sharing holy peace and joy within our families, sharing family prayer on a regular basis, making every meal a holy meal where loving conversations bond family members in unity, sharing family work without grumbling, making love not war, asking forgiveness for past hurts and forgiving one another from the heart, seeking to go all the way for love as Jesus went all the way for love.

"LET US RESOLVE TO MAKE THIS WEEK A HOLY ONE"
MISSISSIPPI TODAY

Jesus promised that if two of us would join our voices in prayer in His name, it would be granted.

ALMOST HOME

Let's get in touch with the need tonight, Church.
Let's be conscious of the need to feel the frustrations, to
feel the grief, to feel the sorrow, to feel the pain, and at
the same time, to feel the hope and the yearning.
I pray to God, my Father, I pray to Jesus, my brother:

For people living with AIDS and
    AIDS-related illnesses,
For families and the friends of people living
    with AIDS and AIDS-related illnesses,
For the people who are afraid, who avoid, who shun
    people with AIDS and AIDS-related illnesses,
For friends who don't know what to say
    and don't know how to say it,
who don't know how to support the ones they love,
For homeless people with AIDS,
For the sick ones who come home to die,
For babies born with AIDS,
For people, especially young people, who are high-risk,
For persons awaiting results from AIDS tests
    and those who are scared to take the test,
For people who feel they have to deny
    that they have AIDS:
    they can't tell friends, they can't tell their families,
For people who know the facts and still are careless
    and irresponsible in their relationships,
For all our loved ones who are in some way touched,
    in some way afflicted by AIDS,

For all my brothers and sisters and fathers and mothers
    and children standing here tonight,
    gathered here today,
    "standing in the need of prayer."
We offer that need as incense before the throne of God.

"HEALING MINISTRY"
ST. STEPHEN'S CATHOLIC CHURCH, MINNEAPOLIS, 1989

One of my favorite prayers these days is just to say, "Thank you, Lord." To look out my window and see the beauty of the tree or the beauty of the sky and to realize all my life I've had food to eat, all my life I've had shelter, I have medical care, I have friends—that God has blessed me. I have been blessed beyond all imagining, and I just want to say, "Thank you, Lord."

ALMOST HOME

I believe that there are kinds of healing. People are praying for healing for me. I want to be healed. I don't know what that means in God's infinite plan, but it's not problematic for me. If it means to heal the body, thank you, God. If it means to heal the spirit, thank you, God. And I know the healing is already happening.

ALMOST HOME

O Lord, help us to be attentive to your commands. Help us to walk in unity. Help us to celebrate who we are and whose we are. Help us to overcome selfishness, anger and violence in our hearts, our homes, our Church, our world. Help us to knock down, pull down, shout down the walls of racism, sexism, classism, materialism, and militarism that divide and separate us. Help us to live as your united people, proclaiming with one voice, our faith, our hope, our love, our joy.

SISTER THEA: SONGS OF MY PEOPLE

For all the times you have delivered us, O Lord, we give you thanks and praise. That you daily lead us from slavery into the freedom of the sons and daughters of God, O Lord, we give you thanks and praise. That you daily lead us toward the Land of Promise, O Lord, we give you thanks and praise. We sing and dance for joy, O Lord, we give you thanks and praise.

SISTER THEA: SONGS OF MY PEOPLE

"THE LORD'S BEEN HERE"
Faith

The Lord's been here and blessed my soul,
The Lord's been here and blessed my soul, O glory,
The Lord's been here and blessed my soul,
The Lord's been here and blessed my soul.

AFRICAN AMERICAN SPIRITUAL

. . .[T]he ones who survived, survived whole physically and mentally and psychologically and whole in their families. They survived because they had faith, faith in some thing, some body, some where. I'm talking about faith to believe in my power. To believe in my determination, to believe in my own wisdom, to believe in myself.

"EXPERIENCING BLACK SPIRITUALITY:
FLYING WITH THE METAPHOR"
SECOND CONFERENCE ON THE SPIRITUAL WOMAN,
MERCY COLLEGE OF DETROIT, 1989

We've come this far by faith. Faith in the rightness of our cause. Faith in loyalty to relationship. Faith in love. The faith was not always appreciated. The vision was not always clear. The relationship sometimes turned sour. But we still had to go on in faith.

"EXPERIENCING BLACK SPIRITUALITY:
FLYING WITH THE METAPHOR"
SECOND CONFERENCE ON THE SPIRITUAL WOMAN,
MERCY COLLEGE OF DETROIT, 1989

That's our history, Church. We've come this far by faith. How? Leaning on the Lord. We've come this far. Can't turn around.

Look inside yourself; look into your heart; look into your life; remember the people who brought you in faith and taught you in faith, who led and fed you in faith. Think about your mama, your grandparents, your godparents, the uncles and the aunts, the brothers and sisters, the grands and great-greats, the ones who led you in the storm, who set a welcoming table for you, who taught you to say "precious Lord take my hand," who convinced you that you were God's child when the world told you you were nobody and would amount to nothing.

"BLACK HISTORY AND CULTURE"
U.S. CATHOLIC HISTORIAN

When we talk about history and culture, we're talking about understanding ourselves, understanding our roots, understanding where we're coming from so we can understand where we are, so we can chart a course toward where we need to go. When we talk about culture, we're just talking about being ourselves, being our best selves, living, claiming and celebrating and sharing the best of the cultures that have formed, uplifted us, and enabled us to survive. We're talking about naming the goals, values, dreams, and aspirations of our hearts, claiming and celebrating them in family and in community where they can do us some good. If you sit there and keep your faith locked up in your heart, it's not going to help any.

"BLACK HISTORY AND CULTURE"
U.S. CATHOLIC HISTORIAN

I can change things. I can make things happen.

INTERVIEW WITH MIKE WALLACE
"60 MINUTES," CBS, 1987

I think the difference between me and some other people is that I am content to do my little bit. Sometimes people think they have to do big things in order to make change. If each one of us would light the candle, we've got a tremendous light.

INTERVIEW WITH MIKE WALLACE
"60 MINUTES," CBS, 1987

Faith. I sometimes wonder how people who don't have faith can deal with sickness, can deal with death, can deal with separation and loss.

SR. THEA: HER OWN STORY

I know in faith that I am weak, and God is strong, and he can accept my poor efforts.

SR. THEA: HER OWN STORY

There were no weapons, no M-16s, no bombs. There was no need for violence. The battle was in God's hands.

God commanded Joshua and the people with the Ark of his Covenanted Presence to encircle Jericho with music, ritual and celebration. God commanded the people to shout—one Lord, one faith, one united people—and the wall came tumbling down. The power of God and the power of a united, believing people prevailed.

When God is on our side, when we walk in faith and hope and love, no wall, no obstacle can stop us.

REFLECTION ON THE SPIRITUAL,
"JOSHUA FIT DE BATTLE OF JERICHO"
SISTER THEA: SONGS OF MY PEOPLE

I believe God made me. I believe God loves me. I believe God has prepared a place. By faith we believe and say that the best is yet to come, and I have to live in that faith.

ALMOST HOME

I believe that if he does not give me what I ask, he gives me something better.

ALMOST HOME

"_O_ MARY, DON'T YOU WEEP, DON'T YOU MOURN"

Hope

૪

O Mary, don't you weep, don't you mourn,
O Mary don't you weep, don't you mourn;
  Pharaoh's army got drowned!
  O Mary, don't you weep.

AFRICAN AMERICAN SPIRITUAL

An amazing number of people are looking for forgiveness. They are looking to forgive themselves. They are looking for ways to let go of the mistakes of the past and the realization that no matter where I come from or what I have done, I am still a good person, and I can still move forward. I need to find the strength and support so that I can make that journey toward my dream and my goal.

INTERVIEW WITH JOE SMITH
WMTV, MADISON, WISCONSIN, 1988

My goal is to share good news. I want people to know that happiness is possible.

INTERVIEW WITH JOE SMITH
WMTV, MADISON, WISCONSIN, 1988

You see, if the voice goes, there are other ways of communication. I would hope that I would have the strength and faith to find them. I am accused of communicating with more than a voice.

INTERVIEW WITH MIKE WALLACE
"60 MINUTES," CBS, 1987

I feel sometimes that I have something I want to do. I have something that I want to say before it's all over.

SR. THEA: HER OWN STORY

Many of us, as we get to a certain age, look back over our lives and we say, "What have I accomplished?" And we ask, "Is it enough?"

SR. THEA: HER OWN STORY

I'm a Franciscan. I want to be an instrument of peace. I want to be an instrument of hope. I want to be an instrument of faith and joy.

SR. THEA: HER OWN STORY

When we remember from whence we came, then we can look into our souls, our Black souls, and testify to that we have seen with Black eyes, heard with Black ears, and understood with African hearts. We can embrace the culture that has enabled us to survive. We can't turn around. We've come too far.

"BLACK HISTORY AND CULTURE"
U.S. CATHOLIC HISTORIAN

Our history is power. We can learn from it. We don't need to make all the mistakes ourselves. If we remember the misery of slavery, the struggles for freedom and Civil Rights, the joys of the past, if we remember how far we have come, our memory is power.

"BLACK HISTORY AND CULTURE"
U.S. CATHOLIC HISTORIAN

Listen! Hear us! While the world is full of hate, strife, vengeance, we sing songs of love, laughter, worship, wisdom, justice, and peace because we are free. Though our forefathers bent to bear the heat of the sun, the strike of the lash, the chain of slavery, we are free. No man can enslave us. We are too strong, too unafraid. America needs our strength, our voices to drown out her sorrows, the clatter of war....Listen! Hear us! We are the voice of Negro America.

THE VOICE OF NEGRO AMERICA ALBUM
THE HOLY CHILD JESUS SINGERS

We have gathered here to remember and to celebrate Dr. Martin Luther King, Jr. But to remember without resolve is empty, and to celebrate without intent is mockery. Martin was a man, not perfect, flawed as we are flawed, determined, dedicated. Martin was an ambassador for justice—an activist, an agitator. Call him what you will, he was willing to speak out, to march, to be jailed, to be cursed, to be spat upon, to be beaten and abused. He was willing to lay down his life for what he believed in. The grandson of a slave, he was able to talk with statesmen and politicians, the rich and the poor, the erudite and the illiterate, old people and little children, garbagemen and farmers, presidents and princes. [He was] preoccupied with that struggle for

freedom, strengthened by his belief that God would lead
the oppressed to freedom.

"MARTIN LUTHER KING:
SEIZE THE VISION" CELEBRATION
MILWAUKEE, WISCONSIN, 1988

But we are not here to celebrate a man; we are here
to celebrate a dream—a dream of freedom, a dream
deeply rooted in the American dream. A dream so vital
that it has drawn people of all lands to these shores.
A dream that dares to say, "Give me your tired, your
poor, your huddled masses yearning to be free." A
dream that all men and women and children can find
life and liberty and happiness and wholeness. Men,
women, children—black, red, white, brown, yellow and
all the colors and hues between—have lived, have died
to make that dream a reality, have died to guarantee
freedom for their children and their children's children
for generations. We are here to celebrate not a man but
a dream—a dream of freedom.

"MARTIN LUTHER KING:
SEIZE THE VISION" CELEBRATION
MILWAUKEE, WISCONSIN, 1988

You can talk about crime in these cities—you can
talk about native rights in a city, in a state that prides
itself on its Indian heritage. You can talk about the
plight of the newest of our refugees. We, if we honor
King, If we are to celebrate King, if we are to live the

dream, we have to work together, all of us, work together for freedom for all of us, for all of God's children. To the affluent among us: Take back to your community the message that if a poor child is disadvantaged, everybody pays. You pay in welfare; you pay in crime; you pay in fear and anxiety. To the poor: Take back to your communities the message that you are able so long as you have your health and strength to demand of this city the opportunity that is yours, the opportunity to learn, the opportunity to earn.

"MARTIN LUTHER KING:
SEIZE THE VISION" CELEBRATION
MILWAUKEE, WISCONSIN, 1988

And if we walk on and talk on and work on and pray on and hold on and love on in faith, we shall overcome. Overcome weakness, overcome fatigue, overcome exhaustion, overcome pain and loneliness, overcome frustration, overcome the prejudices and the stereotypes, the anxieties, the grief, the fear, the negative attitudes—all those barriers and boundaries that keep us apart, overcome racism and classism and sexism and materialism, all those "isms" that keep us apart.

"HEALING MINISTRY"
ST. STEPHEN'S CATHOLIC CHURCH, MINNEAPOLIS, 1989

One day Jesus was going from Galilee to Jerusalem. Many Jews used to avoid Samaria like many Blacks used to avoid Mississippi, go miles around just to keep from passing through.

It was not by chance that Jesus stopped at a town in Samaria named Sychar and paused by the cooling, cleansing, refreshing water. He was tired. He was thirsty. He was hungry. He was human. His body needed rest. But he had work to do. It was not by chance that a teacher, a Jewish rabbi without reproach, requested and accepted the ministry of a Samaritan, a stranger, a sinner, a woman.

The well was deep, and he had no bucket. Jews did not ordinarily talk with Samaritans. Rabbis did not ordinarily speak with women in public. Holy people did not ordinarily consort with public sinners. But Jesus said to her, "Give me to drink." He asked her for a favor. He engaged her in conversation. He helped her to identify her own weakness and her strength. She gave him water from the well that was her Samaria. He, in return, gave her water that became in her a spring of living water giving eternal life. She gave him herself as she was, without subterfuge or guile. He healed her guilt and restored her vitality. He transformed her and used her to bring all of Samaria to his feet.

When I acknowledge myself—my true self—weak, failing, incomplete, inconsequential, yet gifted and capable of transcendence; when I accept my neediness and come just as I am, I too can recognize the Messiah, and with joy I shall go running to *my* city crying, "Come! Come! Come, see a Man told me everything I have done!"

REFLECTION ON THE SONG,
"JESUS MET THE WOMAN AT THE WELL"
SISTER THEA: SONGS OF MY PEOPLE

As we journey together in faith and hope and love, we got to hold on to one another. You got to believe in the essential goodness of all humanity. You are the ones that have to teach the world because some black folks are going to be scared. You have to show that we hold on to one another. We need solidarity when the bullets start to fly. If you're going to talk about black women, you got to talk about death because we're taught that death is a part of life. When the bullets start to fly, when the tear gas comes, when the dogs start barking, when they turn the horses on you, to hold to your sister, to hold to your brother, to hold to your father and your mother, to hold to that strength that you've never seen.

"EXPERIENCING BLACK SPIRITUALITY:
FLYING WITH THE METAPHOR"
SECOND CONFERENCE ON THE SPIRITUAL WOMAN,
MERCY COLLEGE OF DETROIT, 1989

I want to be present. I want to be ready. I want to share what I have—my life, my laughter, my love, my joy. I want to give to you as I receive from you. I want to learn from you. I want my children to learn from you so that we do not repeat mistakes of the past, so that we can grow together and walk together and talk together and live together in love, in joy, in peace forever.

"HEALING MINISTRY"
ST. STEPHEN'S CATHOLIC CHURCH, MINNEAPOLIS, 1989

We are marching towards home, the holy city. The spiritual journey is the journey home. Everybody knows where home is. Home is where you're loved. It's where you belong. Home became for us a figure of paradise. In the hard days and in the trying days, my people prayed for home and for freedom.

"EXPERIENCING BLACK SPIRITUALITY:
FLYING WITH THE METAPHOR"
SECOND CONFERENCE ON THE SPIRITUAL WOMAN,
MERCY COLLEGE OF DETROIT, 1989

"*I* NEVER FELT SUCH LOVE IN MY SOUL BEFO'"

Love

I never felt such love in my soul befo'
I never felt such love in my soul befo'
All the days of my life ever since I been born,
I never felt such love in my soul befo'

AFRICAN AMERICAN SPIRITUAL

During this Holy Week when Jesus gave his life for love, let us truly love one another.

"LET US RESOLVE TO MAKE THIS WEEK A HOLY ONE"
MISSISSIPPI TODAY

Sharing life and faith and love are all our business, but in a special way and by a special calling—giving life, sustaining life, sharing life have always been life for women. Married or single, young or old, rich or poor, in sickness and in health, in life and in death, so long as we have breath and being, we are called to be life-givers and life-nourishers and life-sustainers.

"WOMEN'S DAY" SPEECH
SAINT CLEMENT POPE CHURCH

God's glory is revealed because we love one another across the barriers and boundaries of race, culture, and class.

"COSMIC SPIRITUALITY: NO NEUTRAL GROUND"
1987 NATIONAL CONGRESS OF THE
RELIGIOUS FORMATION CONFERENCE

All my life my mama told me to stand up straight, hold up my head, and speak out. And what happens to the person in formation who dares to? We have the children among us of alienation and anger and frustration, of guilt and shame, men and women with unexpressed hopes and loves and yearnings, with feelings of separation and denial. Children of the universe, we come together in Jesus' name, and the only answer that we can offer to one another is the love that is found in the word of God, the love that is shared and celebrated in Jesus' name. Love, enunciated in a thousand languages, a thousand symbols, a thousand rituals, a thousand ways so that the giftedness and the heritage of the multiplicity of God's people becomes available to all of us and to the church that we call our home….

"COSMIC SPIRITUALITY: NO NEUTRAL GROUND"
1987 NATIONAL CONGRESS OF THE
RELIGIOUS FORMATION CONFERENCE

It has to be love, love that overcomes fear, that shares and makes sure that nobody is hungry, that unites us when we learn about each other, when we share our gifts, when we believe in each other, when we take time to *listen* to each other, and share our stories, our arts, our customs, our traditions, when we break bread together.

"TRUSTING THE PROPHETIC CALL,"
CREATION MAGAZINE

That spirit has seen many of our women through the struggle and preserved the desire to live and leave a legacy of love and a new life. They had the coping mechanisms embedded in their spirituality, embedded in the song, embedded in the prayer, and embedded in the story.

"EXPERIENCING BLACK SPIRITUALITY:
FLYING WITH THE METAPHOR"
SECOND CONFERENCE ON THE SPIRITUAL WOMAN,
MERCY COLLEGE OF DETROIT, 1989

African people became African Americans. Relating and communicating, teaching and learning, loving, and expressing faith in the God who loves and saves, they embodied and celebrated themselves and their values, goals, dreams, and relationships.

"BLACK HISTORY AND CULTURE"
U.S. CATHOLIC HISTORIAN

How can we love and embrace the lonely, the fearful, the homeless, the outcast, the rejected, the unwanted, the unrecognized, the poor? How can we witness to the Good News that we are walking together toward Canaan in love?

SISTER THEA: SONGS OF MY PEOPLE

Everyone does not have access. When I say that, I mean [Martin Luther] King was demonstrating for the rights of the poor, he was demonstrating for fair and decent housing, he was demonstrating for opportunities for adequate education. And not just adequate educational opportunity for blacks, but adequate education for all the children, for all the young men and women. He was demonstrating for a land where we could love one another as brothers and sisters and work together for a solution to our common problems.

INTERVIEW WITH JOE SMITH
WMTV, MADISON, WISCONSIN, 1988

You have a gift. You have a talent. Find your gift, find your talent and use it. You can make this world better just by letting your light shine and doing your part. You can help somebody just by caring about somebody, just by loving somebody. And then when you get through showing them how much you love them, sometimes folks need to hear it, so make sure you tell them, I love you, I love you, I love you. I really, really, really, really love you!

SR. THEA: HER OWN STORY

Love sustains me.

SR. THEA: HER OWN STORY

I find myself much willing and much more eager to tell people that I love them. I find myself much more eager to tell them what they mean in my life.

ALMOST HOME

That's all we've got to do: love the Lord, to love our neighbor. Amen. Amen. Amen. Amen.

"TO BE BLACK AND CATHOLIC"
ADDRESS TO THE U.S. CATHOLIC BISHOPS, JUNE 1989

"ℒITTLE DAVID, PLAY ON YOUR HARP"

Black Spirituality and Songs of My People

Little David, play on your harp,
Hal-le-lu! Hal-le-lu!
Little David Play on your harp,
Hal-le-lu!

AFRICAN AMERICAN SPIRITUAL

Black spirituality is contemplative. To contemplate the living word in the silence of the midnight hour. To contemplate the living word while you're washing your dishes in the sink. To contemplate the living word in the time of trouble and then share that word because black spirituality is communal. Black spirituality is joyful in the time of trouble. Black spirituality is holistic.

"EXPERIENCING BLACK SPIRITUALITY:
FLYING WITH THE METAPHOR"
SECOND CONFERENCE ON THE SPIRITUAL WOMAN,
MERCY COLLEGE OF DETROIT, 1989

Black sacred song is soulful song—

1. *holistic:* challenging the full engagement of mind, imagination, memory, feeling, emotion, voice, and body;
2. *participatory:* inviting the worshipping community to join in contemplation, in celebration and in prayer;
3. *real:* celebrating the immediate concrete reality of the worshipping community—grief or separation, struggle or oppression, determination or joy— bringing that reality to prayer within the community of believers;
4. *spirit-filled:* energetic, engrossing, intense;
5. *life-giving:* refreshing, encouraging, consoling, invigorating, sustaining.

"THE GIFT OF AFRICAN AMERICAN SACRED SONG"
LEAD ME, GUIDE ME:
THE AFRICAN AMERICAN CATHOLIC HYMNAL

From the African Mother Continent, African men and women, through the Middle Passage, throughout the Diaspora, to the Americas, carried the African gift and treasure of sacred song. To the Americas, African men and women brought sacred songs and chants that reminded them of their homelands and that sustained them in separation and in captivity, songs to respond to all life situations, and the ability to create new songs to answer new needs.

"THE GIFT OF AFRICAN AMERICAN SACRED SONG"
LEAD ME, GUIDE ME:
THE AFRICAN AMERICAN CATHOLIC HYMNAL

Black sacred song has been at once a source and an expression of Black faith, spirituality and devotion. By song, our people have called the Spirit into our hearts, homes, churches, and communities. Seeking to enrich our liturgies and lives with the gift of sacred songs, we pray: "Spirit, Sweet Holy Spirit, fall afresh on me."

"THE GIFT OF AFRICAN AMERICAN SACRED SONG"
LEAD ME, GUIDE ME:
THE AFRICAN AMERICAN CATHOLIC HYMNAL

Each spiritual is in its own way a prayer—of yearning or celebration, of praise, petition, or contemplation, a simple lifting of heart, mind, voice, and life to God.

SISTER THEA: SONGS OF MY PEOPLE

When I was a child in Canton, Mississippi, my people sang the songs of faith—songs of Adam and Eve, Cain and Abel, Noah, Moses, David, and Jesus. The songs of faith were passed on, taught, learned, and prayed in an environment of love and celebration. I learned them from Mama, who sang me to sleep, who sang for me and with me in so many special and well-remembered moments; from Mother Rica who gathered twenty-five or thirty children around her in her warm home and sang faith songs that called forth energy and enthusiasm, that invited bodily response, that were fun; from Mrs. Ward, our next-door neighbor, who sang as she worked her garden or hung out wash and fed her chickens, who hummed as she walked down the street; from other children who sang as they played church and baptism and funeral, or as they sang for simple entertainment and joy; from Sayde and Earnest Garrett and the other Garrett brothers who gathered around our piano and sang with us for hours whenever they came to visit; from all the church folks who sang, played instruments, and danced, or who in their faces and bodies reflected the power and beauty of the songs of faith. Sharing the songs of faith bonded us in family and church. Sharing the songs brought hope and consolation and joy.

SISTER THEA: SONGS OF MY PEOPLE

The old folks never wondered if Jonah was real or if the whale was real. They knew the Jonah story was eternal *truth—truth* that no man or woman or little child can hide from the power of an all-seeing, all-knowing, all-powerful God. "You can run but you can't hide." *Truth*—that God will save and deliver: "Didn't my Lord deliver Jonah from the belly of the whale?" *Truth*—that happiness is found only in following God's all-perfect Will: "In God's Will is our peace."

Jonah tried to run away from God, but God did not abandon him. The Jonah story reminds us that God will not forsake us and that God is able to work his Holy Will.

Our God is still in the business of saving. He calls you as he called Jonah to speak the prophetic word. What is God asking of you today? Where is God sending you today? In what ways have you tried to escape his Will?

REFLECTION ON THE PROPHET JONAH
SISTER THEA: SONGS OF MY PEOPLE

Separated from home and family, enslaved and frustrated, lonely and in pain, my ancestors called out to God in longing and in song. What does a good mother do for her child? A child that is truly motherless had no one—no mother, no grandmother, no sister, or father, or friend to mother him.

What is a motherless child? When have you felt like a motherless child? Listen to your own feelings. Bring them to full consciousness before the Lord. Let them be your prayer. How do we make one another feel like motherless children? If you feel like a motherless child, what can you do? If your father/mother/grandparents/husband/wife/child/neighbor/friend/lover feels like a motherless child, what can you do? What will you do today to bring real joy to some motherless child?

REFLECTION ON THE SPIRITUAL,
"SOMETIMES I FEEL LIKE A MOTHERLESS CHILD"
SISTER THEA: SONGS OF MY PEOPLE

I did not realize that the songs would bring to me and to those I love comfort in sorrow, solace in grief, refuge in time of trouble, relief even from physical pain—always strength and hope, peace and joy.

SISTER THEA: SONGS OF MY PEOPLE

"GIVE ME JESUS"
Jesus and Justice

❦

I heard my mother say, I heard my mother say,
I heard my mother say, "Give me Jesus."
Give me Jesus,
Give me Jesus,
You may have all this world,
Give me Jesus.

AFRICAN AMERICAN SPIRITUAL

Some would say that the dream has become a nightmare. We have definitely moved forward in terms of following the dream and celebrating the dream. The legal machinery is in order. The nation, as an institutional and constitutional reality, has recognized the validity of what [Martin Luther] King called the "check" that had been written, not just for black people, but for all people who have come here to claim the heritage and to claim the dream.

INTERVIEW WITH JOE SMITH
WMTV, MADISON, WISCONSIN, 1988

There are old people who have worked hard all their lives who don't have adequate income, who don't have adequate housing, who don't have enough food to eat, who don't have medical care. The complexion of the poor is changing. It used to be if you could do something, you could get a job. But now in this nation, there are people who have education and training, but are unemployed.

INTERVIEW WITH JOE SMITH
WMTV, MADISON, WISCONSIN, 1988

When Martin Luther King, Jr., was in my house where I live, I was in Wisconsin. I missed it. My friends and neighbors were there. They were present when he came into my little three-mile town and sat down with the people of my little town because they, too, were important. Although they were poor, although they were oppressed, although they didn't have ways and means to effect change, he saw in my folks potential. Because of the inspiration he brought, people were able to stand up and claim their dignity, to make an impact on the government and effect change.

INTERVIEW WITH JOE SMITH
WMTV, MADISON, WISCONSIN, 1988

I didn't like drinking water out of the "colored" fountain when the bowl was broken and the white folks had the cold water. I didn't enjoy traveling and going for miles and miles and being unable to use a restroom because the restrooms were for white people. I didn't enjoy hearing a seventeen-year old white girl being called "Miss Smith" and my fifty-year old mother being called "Mary." But we never thought that we had power to effect change. What King did for us was to help us realize that the Constitution was on our side, that the American dream was on our side, that there were good caring people within this nation who did not know what was going on in some of these situations, that well-meaning people were doing racist things because they, too, were in this system that they did not question. And King began to raise the questions, and he helped us to raise the questions. And he began to work with the local leadership, and he taught us.

INTERVIEW WITH JOE SMITH
WMTV, MADISON, WISCONSIN, 1988

Poor little Jesus, born poor, born rejected, born far away from home. "Mary's Baby didn't have no cradle. Didn't have no hotel room." And even at his birth, loomed large the Shadow of the cross. He came to save the poor and lowly. He, in his flesh, has borne our sorrow. He became like us in all things but sin.

SISTER THEA: SONGS OF MY PEOPLE

It didn't matter to Mary and Joseph that their child was born in a stable. They took Jesus to the Temple anyway. It didn't matter to Mary and Joseph that their child was ridiculed by those who didn't appreciate his heritage. They took Jesus to the Temple anyway. It didn't matter to Mary and Joseph that their child would have to journey to Jerusalem without the comfort of a fine carriage or the distinction of a royal robe. They took Jesus to the Temple anyway. It didn't matter to Mary and Joseph that when they got to the Temple it was only a simple old man and a feeble old woman who recognized the presence of God in their child. They didn't need the recognition of the high priest or the approval of the chief magistrate to know that Jesus was a gift from God.

ST. COLUMBA CATHOLIC CHURCH
FEAST OF THE PRESENTATION OF JESUS IN THE TEMPLE

When Jesus is among us, to work among us miracles of transformation and miracles of love, there is no neutral ground. Neutral ground becomes loving ground; loving ground becomes holy ground; holy ground becomes Kingdom ground. We are the children of the cosmos, the children of the universe.

"COSMIC SPIRITUALITY: NO NEUTRAL GROUND"
1987 NATIONAL CONGRESS OF THE
RELIGIOUS FORMATION CONFERENCE

We recoil before the atrocities of war, gang crime, domestic violence and catastrophic illness. Unless we personally and immediately are touched by suffering, it is easy to read scripture and to walk away without contacting the redemptive suffering that makes us holy. The reality of the Word falls on deaf ears. Let us take time this week to be present to someone who suffers. Sharing the pain of a fellow human will enliven scripture and help us enter into the holy mystery of the redemptive suffering of Christ.

"LET US RESOLVE TO MAKE THIS WEEK A HOLY ONE"
MISSISSIPPI TODAY

Let us praise the Lord with our whole heart and soul and mind and strength, uniting with the suffering church throughout the world—in Rome and Northern Ireland, in Syria and Lebanon, in South Africa and Angola, India and China, Nicaragua and El Salvador, in Washington, DC, and Jackson, MS. Let us break bread together; let us relive the holy and redemptive mystery. Let us do it in memory of him, acknowledging in faith his real presence upon our altars.

"LET US RESOLVE TO MAKE THIS WEEK A HOLY ONE"
MISSISSIPPI TODAY

Let us resolve to make this week holy by sharing holy peace and joy with the needy, the alienated, the lonely, the sick and afflicted, the untouchable. Let us unite our sufferings, inconveniences and annoyances with the suffering of Jesus. Let us stretch ourselves, going beyond our comfort zones to unite ourselves with Christ's redemptive work.

"LET US RESOLVE TO MAKE THIS WEEK A HOLY ONE"
MISSISSIPPI TODAY

We unite ourselves with Christ's redemptive work when we reconcile, when we make peace, when we share the good news that God is in our lives, when we reflect to our brothers and sisters God's healing, God's forgiveness, God's unconditional love.

"LET US RESOLVE TO MAKE THIS WEEK A HOLY ONE"
MISSISSIPPI TODAY

"DONE MADE MY VOW TO THE LORD"

"Each one, Teach one!"

Done made my vow to the Lord,
And I never will turn back.
I will go, I shall go,
To see what the end will be.

AFRICAN AMERICAN SPIRITUAL

We get out of this situation that we are in by demanding of ourselves, demanding of the body politic, demanding of the public sector that we put high priority on the education of our children and on our youth. When I say education, I mean academic education, fiscal education, vocational education, parenting education, moral and value education, cultural education; we need a total educational package, and we need to make it available to everybody. And it's your responsibility, it's my responsibility—how can we impact the country in such a way that we get a clear message to our elected leadership that this is what must be?

INTERVIEW WITH JOE SMITH
WMTV, MADISON, WISCONSIN, 1988

All I want to say is that everyone has a responsibility. We need to teach little children—the little five-year-old, the little four-year-old—that they can change things; they can make life better for themselves and for their family and for their country. And even though they can't vote at this time, they can be involved and participatory and contributing citizens.

INTERVIEW WITH JOE SMITH
WMTV, MADISON, WISCONSIN, 1988

Teaching at all levels: How do we teach the poor
that they can change their lives? How do we raise up
the young men and young women with the kind of
confidence in themselves that says, "I am somebody;
I am special"? Even if I am slow, even if I have a drug
problem, even if my parents are gone, even if I don't
have money, I'm somebody. And there are resources
available in my community, and I have to reach out and
grab those resources. And I say that of your child, how
do we teach the children?

INTERVIEW WITH JOE SMITH
WMTV, MADISON, WISCONSIN, 1988

I learned because there were people inside my family
and outside my family who were willing to help me, to
give me a chance, to give me an opportunity. And I
know poor people who would use their money to put
shoes on somebody else's child's feet, who would feed
anyone who came into their home. I believe we have
to return to some of the old value systems. If you know
something, teach somebody. If you know how to read,
teach somebody. If you can fix a car, teach somebody. If
you know how to clean a room, teach somebody. If you
know how to run a computer, teach somebody. If you're
a radiologist, let somebody see, let somebody learn what
you do, and try to inspire somebody. Not only to take
your place, but to surpass you in serving humanity.

INTERVIEW WITH JOE SMITH
WMTV, MADISON, WISCONSIN, 1988

My approach is: teach me. I will learn. I want to learn. I want to keep on learning until I die. But I also want to teach. I want to accept your gifts. Please share your treasures with me, but I also want to share my treasures with you.

SR. THEA: HER OWN STORY

I found high school teaching to be most taxing. I enjoyed it, but it was the hardest for me. You see, I was young when I started to teach high school. I was coming back to my hometown in Mississippi; there was a desperation in my teaching. There was an urgency in my teaching. I came home saying, "You've got to learn!"

SR. THEA: HER OWN STORY

One of the things I learned about students in college is that so many come there programmed to find out what the teacher wants and what the teacher wants them to think and what the teacher wants them to say. I say you don't have to do that. You don't have to be afraid. Think for yourself. Your opinion is as good as mine. So long as you support your opinion by evidence, it is as valid as mine. That was my approach. You've got it, then use it.

SR. THEA: HER OWN STORY

If you figure something out for yourself, does that say there is no God? No, because God gave you the life and ability to think for yourself.

SR. THEA: HER OWN STORY

When we come together from our various spiritual perspectives, we learn from one another. From my Native sisters I learn a spirituality that lives in harmony with nature and with nature's God. I learn African ways of expressing feelings and passions and emotions and frustrations and yearnings influenced by the ignominy of the passage and our experience of slavery in the Americas.

"EXPERIENCING BLACK SPIRITUALITY:
FLYING WITH THE METAPHOR"
SECOND CONFERENCE ON THE SPIRITUAL WOMAN,
MERCY COLLEGE OF DETROIT, 1989

And you know what they used to say in the old days—if you know so much and you are so smart—each one teach one!

"MARTIN LUTHER KING:
SEIZE THE VISION" CELEBRATION
MILWAUKEE, WISCONSIN, 1988

My daddy was convinced that if you could read, you could do anything. And I think he passed that conviction on to me.

INTERVIEW WITH JOE SMITH
WMTV, MADISON, WISCONSIN, 1988

"*I* Know the Lord's Laid His Hands on Me"

Witnessing

❧

O, I know the Lord,
I know the Lord,
I know the Lord's laid his hands on me.

AFRICAN AMERICAN SPIRITUAL

The Word of God became Incarnate. We are called to preach that word day by day by day—in our homes, in our families, in our neighborhood—to bear witness, to testify, to shout it from the rooftops, with our lives.

"WOMEN'S DAY" SPEECH
SAINT CLEMENT POPE CHURCH

The celebrant enunciates the Gospel in the idiom of the people, with drama, energy and intensity. His message relates to their daily lives—poverty, racism, black pride and family values, support for the hungry, the example of Martin Luther King.

"LET THE CHURCH SAY, 'AMEN!'"
EXTENSION MAGAZINE

I invite all of you to pause a moment and bring to mind the women who gave you life, who nurtured you, who gave you light and laughter and faith and love. Did those women preach, did they teach, did they testify, did they witness?

"WOMEN'S DAY" SPEECH
SAINT CLEMENT POPE CHURCH

Ladies, we are called to plant the Word in the minds and hearts and souls of our children, husbands, lovers, fathers, brothers, uncles, nephews, and friends. We don't have to worry about deception and hypocrisy....They know when our witness is the fruit of our effort and struggle and sincerity.

God has called to us to speak the word that is Christ, that is truth, that is salvation. And if we speak that word in love and faith, with patience and prayer and perseverance, it will take root. It does have power to save us. Call one another! Testify! Teach! Act on the Word! Witness!

"WOMEN'S DAY" SPEECH
SAINT CLEMENT POPE CHURCH

Black spirituality demands not only that you believe and that you hope and that you love. It also demands that you witness and you testify. Testifying: it's part of the spirituality. It's also affirming. It's also encouraging. That spirituality is participatory. It is having people say to me what God is for them, to believe and to share that faith in communion in the family, in a relationship, in love.

"EXPERIENCING BLACK SPIRITUALITY:
FLYING WITH THE METAPHOR"
SECOND CONFERENCE ON THE SPIRITUAL WOMAN,
MERCY COLLEGE OF DETROIT, 1989

Let us be practical, reaching out across the boundaries of race and class and status to help somebody, to encourage and affirm somebody, offering to the young an incentive to learn and grow, offering to the downtrodden resources to help themselves. May our fasting be the kind that saves and shares with the poor, that actually contacts the needy, that gives heart to heart, that touches and nourishes and heals.

"LET US RESOLVE TO MAKE THIS WEEK A HOLY ONE"
MISSISSIPPI TODAY

Oh no, I don't preach! I witness. I testify. I share the Good News of the Lord Jesus Christ. The priests can preach. You know women don't preach in the Catholic Church.

INTERVIEW WITH MIKE WALLACE
"60 MINUTES," CBS, 1987

Who you gonna listen to first, the official preacher or your own mama? I think women have always had influence within our own communities and always will. So if I can't preach in the Church, that's all right with me. I can preach in the school. I can preach in the home. I can preach on the bus. I can preach on the train. I can preach on the street.

INTERVIEW WITH MIKE WALLACE
"60 MINUTES," CBS, 1987

I try to get them to work with their bodies. Many of our priests in their training for preaching didn't do much body work. So I use techniques of relaxation, I use techniques of rhythm, techniques of communication and expression that come from the black community.

INTERVIEW WITH MIKE WALLACE
"60 MINUTES," CBS, 1987

I see my role as a sister, as a Franciscan Sister of Perpetual Adoration, as the role of every Christian—to share the Good News of the Lord Jesus Christ, to be Church.

SR. THEA: HER OWN STORY

I remember once saying to a priest, "I really enjoyed your sermon," and he was insulted. He told me that you are not supposed to enjoy a sermon. It is supposed to feed your soul and your spirit. I said, "Excuse me!" I was used to a church where the preacher promised that you would have a good time in the Lord!

SR. THEA: HER OWN STORY

Children, Mothers, Fathers, Sisters, Brothers, go!

There is a song that will never be sung unless you sing it. There is a story that will never be told unless you tell it. There is a joy that will never be shared unless you bear it.

Go tell the world. Go preach the Gospel. Go teach the Good News.

God is. God is love. God is with us. God is in our lives.

SISTER THEA: SONGS OF MY PEOPLE

"DEEP RIVER"
Living With
Suffering and Dying

Deep river,
My home is over Jordan,
Deep river, Lord,
I want to cross over into campground.

AFRICAN AMERICAN SPIRITUAL

Cast out of paradise, exiled and troubled, humanity longed for *home*.

Brought out of Egypt, wandering through desert and wilderness, God's people longed for *home*, the Promised Land across Jordan that would flow with milk and honey.

In the days of slavery, separated from kin and country, my ancestors longed for *home*.

Home is where love is, where you are nurtured and sheltered and challenged and comforted. *Home* is where you are fed and where tears are wiped away, where you find security, where you know you belong.

For slaves who longed so passionately for home, home became a figure of heaven, the heavenly City, where there would be no separation, no death, no auction block, no moaning, no weeping or wailing, no sorrow, no loss. The big extended-family, after-harvest gathering at camp ground, where loved ones who lived and worked apart could pray and sing and walk and talk and eat and laugh and cry together became a figure of the New Jerusalem, the Holy City where all will know we are His because we love one another.

As we journey together toward our eternal home, how can we be home for one another?

SISTER THEA: SONGS OF MY PEOPLE

I went through a struggle in the beginning: I didn't know what to pray for; I didn't know how to approach it. A part of my upbringing has said I want to make heaven my home, and this world is not my home, and I want to go home. And when I first found that I had cancer, I was told by a doctor that I might have a few months or maybe a few years to live. I thought that might be neat, go home, be free. But my friends and my students and people who loved me convinced me that there was more to living than dying. And I came to a place in my own life where my prayer has been, "Lord, let me live until I die." I don't know what that means, but what it means doesn't really matter in terms of time. What I say is I want to live fully, I want to give fully. I want to be the best person I can during the time that I have.

ALMOST HOME

Part of my approach to my illness has been to say I want to choose life, I want to keep going, I want to live fully until I die.…

I don't know what the future holds. In the meantime, I am making a conscious effort to learn to live with discomfort, and, at the same time, to go about my work. I find that when I am involved in the business of life, when I'm working with people, particularly with children, I feel better. A kind of strength and energy comes with that.

"LORD, LET ME LIVE TILL I DIE,"
PRAYING MAGAZINE

Life for a while and then death. It's as simple as that. When I first found out I had cancer, I didn't know what to pray for. I didn't know if I should pray for healing or life or death. Then, I found peace in praying for what my folks call "God's perfect will." As it evolved, my prayer has become, "Lord, let me live until I die." By that I mean I want to live, love and serve fully until death comes. If that prayer is answered, if I am able to live until I die, how long really doesn't matter. Whether it's just a few months or a few years is really immaterial.

I grew up with people who believed you could serve the Lord from a sickbed or a deathbed. The great commandment is to love the Lord your God with your whole heart, your whole soul, your whole mind, and all your strength. As long as I have my mental facility, I want to keep on loving. I want to keep on serving. That's what I hope to be about.

My illness has helped me to realize how fragile our hold on life is. I always thought I was going to live to be an old woman, like my mother and my father and all the other old people I knew and was close to when I was a child. But I no longer think that. My time isn't long. Now I just want to find ways to make the most of the time I have left.

"LORD, LET ME LIVE TILL I DIE,"
PRAYING MAGAZINE

Yes, I moan sometimes, I sing sometimes. When I'm sick and don't have the internal resources to pray as I would like, I sing or moan or hum. Because the songs are so familiar, it is an easy way to pray, to unite myself with God. When I have pain, I find it goes away when I hum or sing.…It's a lesson I learned from my people and my heritage.

"LORD, LET ME LIVE TILL I DIE,"
PRAYING MAGAZINE

I was taught that if I could find inner peace, inner strength and inner composure, I could bear sorrow, I could bear illness, I could bear death. I believe that teaching, and I have tried in my life to learn to live the teaching. It's a day-by-day-by-day decision that I want to live joyfully. I want to be good news for other people. I want to feel good about myself. I want you to feel good about me. I want to help you feel good about yourself. I try to smile, I try to laugh, I try to find the sources of strength and joy. I want people to remember me as smiling. I want people to remember me as caring about them, no matter what happens to me.

SR. THEA: HER OWN STORY

When I go before Judgment, I want to be able to say that I have really tried. I've done my best.

SR. THEA: HER OWN STORY

I grew up in that kind of world in which life and death was a part of the cycle of reality that was a part of God's plan that was good.

ALMOST HOME

Sister "Dort" Kundinger, FSPA, has borne the frustration. She's helped me bear pain. She has just been there. I think sometimes people do not realize how much strength and how much help and how much support a person who is ill can derive just by the presence of somebody who loves and somebody who cares and somebody who understands.

ALMOST HOME

We are a pilgrim people traveling together in sorrow and joy toward that land of promise. Where there will be no more sorrow, no more moaning, no more weeping and wailing, no more goodbye, but just hello.

ALMOST HOME

I worry about the kinds of personality changes that come with illness. If I can't deal with it, I sing. I find that for some miraculous reason, if I can sing, I can cope. I like to moan sometimes....it makes me feel better.

ALMOST HOME

In my life I've found laughter helpful, so I laugh.

ALMOST HOME

With the little time you have, you have to live it well; you have to live the best you can.

ALMOST HOME

I'm afraid of pain. I'm afraid of helplessness. I'm afraid of a life where I'm not able to serve.

ALMOST HOME

I think that cancer causes one to re-evaluate priorities. You begin to have some very different perceptions about what's important in life and what isn't important. Many things that I used to worry about, I realize don't matter any more. I find myself more patient and more tolerant of small things. I think I have a different sense of time. I think all of my relationships, including my relationship to God, are most important to me.

ALMOST HOME

Time really doesn't matter. When it is over, it will be all over. I want people who love me to know that I tried to choose life, and I did it for myself, but I also did it for them.

ALMOST HOME

. . .In the future I've been required to cut back my schedule and build more time for rest and recovery. I have to learn that the body is no longer 18 years old and needs adequate maintenance. But that's all right, too. We know that God has been good to me.

And my friends have, too. Thank you for your concern, prayers, calls, visits, letters, cards, fruit, flowers, car rides, food service, blood gifts, and pitching in to help with whatever. My friends are wonderful and wonderfully affirming and encouraging. God bless and reward you all.

LETTER TO FRIENDS, MARCH 1988

. . .My doctors are all conferring to decide if the best treatment will be radiation, chemotherapy, surgery, or some combination....

I had to cancel all my January commitments, and what February will bring, God knows.

I ask your prayers. I'm very weak, but my spirits are good and I'm trying to keep on keeping on.

Again, I'm sorry for being so slow to respond to your generosity.

Love, Thea

LETTER TO FRIENDS, JANUARY 22, 1990

I say what I want on my tombstone is, "She tried." I want people to remember that I tried to love the Lord and that I tried to love them, and how that computes is immaterial.

ALMOST HOME

If you use this at the end [of the video], I just want to say goodbye. It's been good to know you, and keep on keeping on.

ALMOST HOME

$\mathscr{E}$PILOGUE

An African proverb from the Congo says, "Let him [or her] speak who has seen with his [or her] eyes." Thea possessed big, bright eyes that drew people to her. She had visionary eyes: eyes that had seen both joy and sorrow in her fifty-two years of life, eyes that saw the best in people, eyes that gave us hope for ourselves and hope for the Church. She had eyes that remained strong, as her body grew weak from battling cancer. Yet Thea continued to witness to what she had seen, as long as she had a voice to speak.

The words of Thea Bowman inspired and em-powered generations of people across creeds, cultures, socio-economic backgrounds, academic achievement, and spiritual experiences. Her voice simultaneously challenged, encouraged, and instilled hope—in essence, it was a clarion call to make Christ present in all we say and do. Thea wanted all those who knew her and loved her to continue to be good news for one another and especially for those who are marginalized, alienated, oppressed, and hopeless.

Sister Thea Bowman, FSPA, PhD, went home like "a shooting star" in her beloved Canton, Mississippi, family home at 136 Hill Street on March 30, 1990. Her name now graces both parochial and public schools, community centers, a health center, a wellness institute, religious education centers, a women's leadership center, a center for social service and social action, a family transitional housing program, scholarships, an educational foundation, and even a movie theatre! She has been memorialized in paintings, icons, prayer services and prayer cards, retreats, catechism books, gospel choirs, a Gospel Mass setting, and church shrines. Babies have been named after her, and young ladies have claimed her name at confirmation, all to attest that her living was not in vain and that she made a difference. Sister Eva Lumas, SSS, D.Min., proclaims: "She is the Church, black and non-black. She is Christianity two thousand years old, two thousand years young."

Thea wrote these final words to me a few months before her passing. While personal, Thea's words were always universal, so I share them with you:

My children, my friends, and my God are the source of my strength. Thanks for being my son and friend, and thanks for helping me to keep on keeping on.
I love you,
Thea

Sources and Permissions

The use of certain writings or speeches of Sr. Thea Bowman in this book has been authorized by the Franciscan Sisters of Perpetual Adoration, La Crosse, Wisconsin, the copyright owner of materials in Sr. Thea's literary estate. Their permission and participation is gratefully acknowledged.

The publisher and the compiler also express gratitude to the following for granting permission to reproduce material of which they are the publisher or copyright holder. Excerpts from: *Lead Me, Guide Me: The African American Catholic Hymnal*, © 1987 G.I.A. Publications, Inc., Chicago, IL, used with permission of publisher; *Sister Thea, Songs of My People*, compilation © 1989 St. Paul Books & Media, used with permission of Pauline Books and Media, Boston, MA; "Let Us Resolve to Make This Week a Holy One," *Mississippi Today* (Feb. 1990), reprinted with permission of *Mississippi Catholic*, Jackson, MS; *Sr. Thea: Her Own Story* (DVD), © 1990 Oblate Media and Communication, Florissant, MO, used with permission of the publisher; *Sister Thea Bowman: Almost Home, Living With Suffering & Dying* (DVD), © 2008 Liguori Publications, Liguori, MO, www.liguori.org.

Excerpts from Sr. Thea's interview with Mike Wallace for a 1987 "60 Minutes" telecast are used with permission of CBS News, New York, NY.

Excerpts from Sr. Thea's 1988 WMTV interview with Joe Smith are used with permission of WMTV, Madison, Wisconsin.

Reprinted with grateful acknowledgment:

Excerpts from: A chapter authored by Sr. Thea entitled, "Religious and Cultural Variety: Gift to Catholic Schools," from *The Non-Catholic in the Catholic School*, Washington, DC: National Catholic Educational Association (Dept. of Religious Education), 1984: 20-25; *Families, Black and Catholic, Catholic and Black: Readings, Resources and Family Activities*, Thea Bowman, ed., © 1985 United States Catholic Conference, Inc., Washington, DC; "Trusting the Prophetic Call," *Creation* (Nov.–Dec. 1989): 19-21 (Catherine Browning's interview with Sister Thea Bowman); "Let the Church Say, 'Amen!'" *Extension* (Mar.–Apr. 1987): 10-11; "Let Me Live Till I Die," *Praying* (Nov.–Dec. 1989): 19-22 (Fabvienen Taylor's interview with Sister Thea); "Black History and Culture," by Sister Thea Bowman, *U.S. Catholic Historian* 7, Nos. 2 and 3 (Spring–Summer 1988): 307-310.

Sr. Thea's comments made in New Orleans, LA, in the address, "Cosmic Spirituality: No Neutral Ground," are reprinted from *Formation in a New Age: Proceedings of the 1987 Religious Formation National Congress* (Washington, DC: Religious Formation Conference).

Sr. Thea's comments in her address to the U.S. Catholic Bishops on June 17, 1989, are reprinted from "Bishops' Meeting/Sr. Thea Bowman: To Be Black and Catholic," *Origins, CNS Documentary Service* No. 8 (July 6, 1989), vol. 19 © 1989, Catholic News Service, Washington, DC.

Sr. Thea's comments at Mercy College of Detroit, April 1989 are from Thea Bowman, "Experiencing Black Spirituality: Flying with the Metaphor," Second Conference on the Spiritual Woman: And Sarah Laughed.

Sr. Thea's comments on a record album appeared in *The Holy Child Singers: The Voice of Negro America* (LP), Century Records, No. 25920 (Holy Child Jesus High School, Canton, MS, circa 1966).

Sr. Thea's comments on the Feast of the Presentation of Jesus in the Temple were presented at St. Columba Catholic Church.

Sr. Thea's comments on "Healing Ministry" were presented at St. Stephen's Catholic Church, Minneapolis, MN, in 1989.

The excerpt from Sr. Thea's "Women's Day" speech at Saint Clement Pope Church is from her handwritten notes for that speech.

Sr. Thea's comments at the "Martin Luther King: Seize the Vision" Celebration were made in January 1988, in Milwaukee, WI.

About the Author

Maurice J. Nutt, C.Ss.R., D.Min., is an ordained priest and a member of the Congregation of the Most Holy Redeemer—more commonly known as the Redemptorists. Father Nutt is a noted revival, mission, and retreat preacher, both nationally and internationally. He is also director of the Institute for Black Catholic Studies (IBCS) at Xavier University in New Orleans, Louisiana, where he teaches preaching.